MAD about

SWIMMING

JUDITH HENEGHAN

WAYLAND

WAYLAND

Published in paperback in 2016
First published in hardback in 2014 by Wayland
Copyright © Wayland 2014

Wayland, an imprint of
Hachette Children's Group
Part of Hodder & Stoughton
Carmelite House, 50 Victoria Embankment
London EC4Y oDZ

Editor: Nicola Edwards
Design: Rocket Design (East Anglia) Ltd

A catalogue record for this title is available from
the British Library.

Dewey number 797.2'1-dc23

ISBN: 978 0 7502 9460 7
Library e-book ISBN: 978 0 7502 8841 5

Printed in China
10 9 8 7 6 5 4

An Hachette UK company
www.hachette.co.uk
www.hachettechildrens.co.uk

The author and publisher would like to thank the following for allowing their pictures to be reproduced in this publication: Cover (t) Michael Wicks, rest Shutterstock; p4 (t) Shuttterstock.com/ dotshock, (b) Francois Xavier Marit/AFP/Getty Images; p5 (t) Wikimedia Commons, (b) Getty Images; p6 (t) Shuttterstock.com/ mims, (b) Shuttterstock.com/ Krzysztof Wiktor, p7 (t) Shuttterstock.com/ Dick Stada, (b) Shuttterstock.com/ dotshock; p8 (t) Wikimedia Commons, (b and inset) Michael Wicks, p9 Adam Pretty/Getty Images; p10 (t) Shuttterstock.com/ bikeriderlondon, (b) Shuttterstock.com/ Rod Ferris; p11 (t) Shuttterstock.com/ bikeriderlondon, (b) Michael Wicks; p12 Shuttterstock.com/ Iurli Osadchi; p13 (t) Shuttterstock.com/ Paolo Bona, (b) Mark J. Terrill/AP/Press Association; p14 (t) Shuttterstock.com/ Sergey Peterman, (b) Shuttterstock.com/ Willyam Bradberry; p15 Shutterstock.com / Mitch Gunn; p16 (t) Shuttterstock.com/ N Minton; (b) Quinn Rooney/Getty Images; p17 With thanks to Steph Marsh & her daughters and Sudbury Life Saving Club; p18 (t) Shuttterstock.com/ Susan Leggett, (b) Shuttterstock.com/ dotshock; p19 (t) Michael Wicks, (b) Shuttterstock.com/ BrunoRosa; p20 Getty Images/MCT; p21 (t) Shuttterstock.com/ Pavel Sazonov, (b) Shuttterstock.com/ Pavel L Photo and Video; p22 (t) Shuttterstock.com/ Jorg Hackemann, (b) Shuttterstock.com/ Paolo Bona; p23 (t) ChinaFotoPress/ ChinaFotoPress via Getty Images; p24 (t) Shuttterstock.com/ Goran Bogicevic, (b) Shuttterstock.com/ luca85; p25 Shuttterstock.com/ Natursports; p26 (t) Shuttterstock.com/ Krivosheev Vitaly, (b) Shuttterstock.com/ Andrey Armyagov; p27 (t) Shuttterstock.com/ Dudarev Mikhail, (b) Shuttterstock.com/ Vlad61; p28 (t) Shuttterstock.com/ pedalist, (b) Tim Graham/ Getty Images; p29 (t) Shuttterstock.com/ Monkey Business Images, (b) culturalcommunity partnership.org.uk

Every effort has been made to trace the copyright holders. We apologise in advance for any unintentional omissions and would be pleased to insert the appropriate acknowledgements in any future editions of this publication.

Contents

Make a splash!

My family says I'm mad about swimming! I go to the local pool with my friends whenever I can. We swim lengths, practise our diving and always finish with a big game of tag. I've had lessons so I'm quite confident in the water. The pool is where we relax and have fun.

Swimming is a great way to spend active time with your friends.

A sport for all

Swimming is one of the world's most popular sports. It's a great way to keep fit because unlike many activities, it uses all the body's major muscles. Also, once you've learned to swim you can safely participate in loads of other sports such as water polo, kayaking and sailing. Or maybe you'd like to get involved in specialised kinds of swimming such as synchro or scuba diving.

You need to be a strong swimmer to perform underwater gymnastics like this synchronised swimming team from Russia.

A public outdoor pool is sometimes called a lido. The lifeguards help everyone enjoy the water safely.

Where to swim

Your local public pool is a great place to swim, because the lifeguards are trained to keep everyone safe in the water. Pools can be indoor or outdoor, filled with fresh or salt water. Never swim in the sea or in lakes or ponds unless there is a lifeguard on duty and clear information that it is safe to do so. If you aren't a confident swimmer, check the depth before you get in. Make sure the water doesn't come up higher than your waist.

CHECKLIST

You don't need lots of fancy equipment to swim!

- ☑ trunks or a swimsuit
- ☑ a towel
- ☑ a pool
- ☑ a lifeguard
- ❓ Goggles, floats, swim caps and flippers are optional!

THE EXPERT SAYS...

Ellie Simmonds, UK Paralympian gold medallist, says: "The first thing is to enjoy what you do... Give everything you've got and always try your best."

Sink or swim!

This girl isn't swimming, but she is staying afloat by 'treading water' – making small movements with her hands and feet.

When I'm swimming, I feel free. The water takes my weight, so I can move in any direction and even do somersaults. My swimming teacher taught me to float by lying on my back, arms and legs apart in a star shape, tummy and chin pushing up towards the roof. My hands are the only parts that move, but this is just enough to stop me from sinking!

Moving through water

Our bodies have some natural buoyancy, which is why we don't sink if we make regular movements in the water with our hands, arms, feet and legs. Animals that swim well have webbed feet like a frog or muscular tails to push themselves through the water. Many of our swimming strokes are based on animal movements!

This otter has a streamlined shape. It uses its large paws and tail to push itself through the water.

Different strokes

There are four main swimming strokes: breaststroke, front crawl, backstroke and butterfly. Some people prefer to swim using a kind of doggy paddle, but learning a stroke helps you to use your body more efficiently and take part in competitive swimming. The best and safest way to learn is to have lessons in a pool with a qualified instructor.

Using a float as a buoyancy aid helps to keep this girl afloat while she learns to swim.

THE EXPERT SAYS...

Matthew Grevers, US Olympic gold medallist, says: "To warm up before a race, I usually do a series of arm stretches, then leg stretches. I always want to make sure I can put my nose to my knee to make sure my body is loose."

top tip

Swimming is a vigorous form of exercise. Like any exercise, it is important to warm up first. Make sure you stretch properly before you get in the water. This helps you avoid muscle strain and cramp.

Breaststroke

Breaststroke is the first stroke I learned. It's a good one to begin with because you don't have to put your head in the water. You can breathe when you want and also see what's going on around you! Now that I'm more confident with my arm and leg movements I do put my head under. It makes me more streamlined for the glide part of the stroke.

Breaststroke is the oldest known swimming stroke, shown here in ancient cave paintings.

Pushing and pulling

A good breaststroke is all about coordination, timing and rhythm. First your arms and hands move out to the sides to pull you through the water. Next, your legs and feet push against the water with a frog kick, which is the strongest part of this stroke. The final part is the glide, with arms and legs fully extended. Remember to keep your fingers together.

As the legs bend, ready to kick, the arms pull back through the water.

Drag

Breaststroke isn't the fastest stroke because your arms stay under the water the whole time; it is harder to push the body through water than it is to move it through air. Also, moving the arms and legs out to the sides creates more resistance – drag – than other strokes, and slows you down.

More experienced swimmers put their heads underwater during the glide phase between each stroke to reduce drag and make themselves more streamlined. Then they lift their head and shoulders out of the water to breathe and kick out the next stroke.

CHECKLIST

To reduce drag and increase speed, practise the following:

- ☑ fingers together
- ☑ feet turned out during frog kick
- ☑ head in the water with arms against ears during glide phase
- ☑ shoulders, hips and knees at the same level in the water at all times

Christian Sprenger (centre), Australian breaststroke champion, shows how legs and arms stretch out after kicking to allow the body to move through the water with as little resistance as possible.

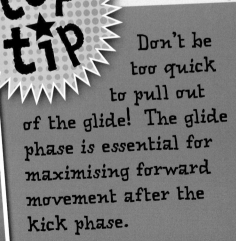

top tip

Don't be too quick to pull out of the glide! The glide phase is essential for maximising forward movement after the kick phase.

Front crawl

Front crawl is fast and streamlined. I need to keep my body as narrow as I can. Most of the work is done by my arms, which pull me through the water. The movements of my arms and legs need to be continuous and smooth so that I move across the pool with as little drag as possible. When I'm swimming well it feels like I'm slicing through the water!

Front crawl is sometimes called 'freestyle'. In a freestyle race, swimmers choose which stroke to swim. Everyone chooses front crawl because it is the fastest!

Breathing

Breathing while swimming front crawl takes a bit of practice. As your arm reaches out of the water, turn your face to that side and breathe in through your mouth. Then put your face back under water to breathe out. Try not to lift your whole head out of the water as this creates drag and slows you down.

Keeping one side of your head in the water while you breathe helps reduce drag and prevent neck strain.

An efficient flutter kick means keeping the knees and ankles loose while kicking from the thigh with as little splash as possible.

The flutter kick

With front crawl, legs should be long and ankles loose. The kicks should start from the thigh and be steady and continuous to keep your body balanced. Try not to bend your knees at more than a 30 degree angle as this slows you down a lot. Start the kick below the water's surface and aim to avoid splashing too much. The kick has no power when your leg is out of the water.

The arm enters the water fingers first, with the elbow slightly bent.

top tip

The arms work hard to pull the body through the water during front crawl. Reach forward so that your fingertips enter the water ahead of you, in line with your shoulder. Don't try to force the water downwards with your hand as this creates drag. Instead, save your energy for pushing the water past your body as your arm pulls back and out.

Backstroke

Backstroke is my favourite stroke. It's a bit like front crawl, but on my back. I can see how fast I'm swimming by keeping my eyes on the ceiling. Breathing is easier too, because my face is always out of the water. Of course, you can't see the pool edge ahead of you, but with a bit of practice, you won't need to.

Keep the arm straight as it passes by the ear and then rotate the wrist so that the little finger enters the water first.

Swim straight

Swimmers use the same flutter kick as for front crawl, kicking between 5 and 7 times for each arm stroke. The arms do most of the work to move you forward, but the legs add stability and keep you in a straight line. Keep your head still, looking up with chin away from your chest. If your head moves around, you may end up swimming in a zig zag!

top tip

Practise counting your strokes (the number of times an arm enters the water) so that you know exactly how many you need to do in a single length before your fingers touch the pool wall.

A good backstroke start is where the push-off is strong and arms and upper body enter the water in a streamlined arch shape.

The backstroke start

Backstroke is the only racing stroke where swimmers always start in the water. Face the pool side, gripping the edge with both hands. Your feet should be pressed against the wall with knees and elbows bent. As your legs push off from the side, raise your arms behind your head, chin back, to make an arch shape with your body. Your hands should be the first part of your upper body to touch the water.

US gold medallist Missy Franklin finishes her race at the 2012 London Olympics. Her whole body, including fingers, is extended as she touches the wall.

THE EXPERT SAYS...

British champion swimmer Karen Pickering says: *"Sitting up in the water is the biggest mistake made in backstroke: if your hips drop too low, your body creates resistance which slows you down. Try and swim with your body close to the surface of the water – imagine you are lying in a bed with your head on a pillow – and push your tummy up to the ceiling, keeping your midriff flat."*

Butterfly

Butterfly gets its name from the movement of the swimmer's arms as they rise like wings out of the water.

Butterfly takes a lot of stamina. You need to have core body strength because instead of using just your arms and legs you use your whole body to propel yourself through the water. It's amazing to watch because the swimmer's head and shoulders surge up above the water while the arms rise out sideways like a pair of wings!

The dolphin kick

The key to a good butterfly stroke is the wave-like movement of the swimmer's body. The legs don't kick separately, but instead move together, up and down, starting from the waist and hips. Most swimmers practise this movement first. They don't add the arm stroke until they are confident with their kick.

The dolphin propels itself through the water by moving its body up and down. This movement gives the 'dolphin kick' its name.

Michael Phelps, US swimmer and winner of 18 Olympic gold medals, says: *"In my opinion the most important part of butterfly training is holding the stroke, making sure you have good technique with hips riding the surface and a strong kick."*

Good coordination

Butterfly may not feel very natural at first, but once you've learned to coordinate your arms with the dolphin kick, it gets easier! Make sure both arms swing and pull at exactly the same time, and kick the legs twice during each arm cycle. The first kick comes as the hands enter the water. The second kick is usually a stronger, deeper one as it has to push the swimmer's head and shoulders up above the water.

top tip

Keep a bottle of water at the pool edge when you're swimming. You sweat just as much as you do for any sport, and it's easy to become dehydrated because you're in the water and don't feel hot.

Safely does it

I use my swimming skills when I go surfing in the summer. I also follow the safety advice. The sea isn't predictable like the pool. You can't see the strong currents below the surface that sweep away from the shore. Even though I'm a confident swimmer, I don't enter the sea unless there are lifeguards who say it is safe to do so. Then my friends and I catch some waves!

These flags show the safe zone for swimming.

Swimmers taking part in open-water challenges need a full support team close by in case they get into difficulty.

Open water

There are lots of places where people swim outdoors but rivers, lakes and ponds can be dangerous. You can't see strong currents or hazards beneath the surface and intense cold can cause muscle cramp. Always obey warning signs and never swim alone or out of your depth. Swimmers attempting big open-water challenges always have support teams and boats near them.

Life saving skills teach you how to swim safely and how to respond in an emergency.

Life-saving skills

One way to stay safe and help others stay safe too is to learn some life-saving skills. Many swimming clubs offer courses and awards. There are lots of different levels depending on your age and swimming ability; it is a great way to improve your swimming technique and feel more confident in the water.

CHECKLIST

Before you get into any kind of water:

☑ Check that there is a lifeguard watching

☑ Check for any hazards or warnings

☑ Check that everyone else with you can swim with confidence

☑ Check the depth before jumping in or diving

top tip

Even if you are a strong swimmer, others may not be. If you visit a private pool without a lifeguard, ask a responsible adult to watch you and be sure to shut any gates or doors so that very young children can't wander in.

Club fun

Swimming meets are exciting events where you can compete yourself and cheer on your friends in their races.

I joined my local swimming club six months ago. Now I train with them twice a week. I've learned to do a racing dive and my tumble turns are improving all the time. Last month I entered my first inter-club competition, called a 'meet', which was pretty amazing. But for me, the best thing about joining a club is making loads of friends – we're all mad about swimming!

Training

As with any sport, the more you practice, the better you become. Training with a club means you can practise with other swimmers at the same level as you, and of course there's a coach to guide and teach you. You'll also have access to lots of information about general fitness, equipment and diet.

Clubs aren't just for competitions. Your coach will teach you new skills.

The tumble turn

The tumble turn

In a race, swimmers finishing one length need to begin the next as quickly as possible. However, there are rules about what makes a 'legal' turn. For breaststroke and butterfly, swimmers must touch the side with both hands before turning. For front crawl, swimmers are allowed to touch it only with their feet. This type of turn is called a tumble turn and the extra speed it gives is vital for competitive swimming.

CHECKLIST

For a tumble turn:
- ☑ swim towards the wall
- ☑ forward somersault
- ☑ push off from wall with feet
- ☑ twist onto front again
- ☑ streamlined glide
- ☑ swim away from the wall

THE EXPERT SAYS...

US gold medallist Missy Franklin says: *"I love swimming and enjoy every practice with my teammates. Travel meets are so much fun as we get to know each other better and become closer. It also is exciting developing friendships with swimmers from other teams from all over the country and the world. Besides all that, I just love the water. It is my element."*

In it to win it!

I love the buzz of a race. It feels good to know I've trained hard and practised all the different aspects – my entry, my stroke, my turns and my finish. Often we travel to other swimming clubs and there's always a great atmosphere with everyone cheering from the poolside. It spurs me on to swim my fastest times.

Relay races

Swimmers can compete as teams as well as individually. The relay race is one of the most exciting forms of competitive swimming as it involves four team-members swimming in turn. A relay medley is when each team-member swims a different stroke.

The judges watch closely to make sure that no team-member enters the water before the previous team-member has touched the side. If you set off too early, your team will be disqualified!

The buzz of the crowd at a race meet, such as here at the 2012 Olympics, can help swimmers achieve their best times.

Ellie Simmonds, UK Paralympian gold medallist, says: "I love the feeling of a race, the relief when you touch the end of the pool, the excitement when you look back at the time board."

THE EXPERT SAYS...

Every second counts

Races are often won by a fraction of a second. Increasingly, clubs are introducing touch pad technology that registers the exact moment at which a swimmer touches the side at the end of a race because this is more accurate than the judges' eyesight. Competitive swimmers often choose to keep their hair short or wear swim caps and 'body suits' to reduce drag and ensure their bodies are as streamlined as possible in the water.

This swimmer's cap and body suit help her to swim as fast as possible when she races.

top tip

The racing dive

A powerful, streamlined dive can give you the edge in a race. Keep your knees slightly bent and push off hard, extending your arms and legs as you travel towards the water. The top of your head should enter the water through the 'hole' made by your hands. Once your body is in the water, let the glide carry your forward before you start your first stroke.

Diving in

Before you learn to dive you'll need to show you are a confident swimmer in deep water.

My cousin Maya is a great diver. She goes to a diving club because you have to learn how to dive safely. A good dive takes a lot of concentration – you're aiming to enter in a straight, vertical position with as little splash as possible. Feet should be together with toes pointed. Maya's been diving for three years; she's strong and flexible and her coach is teaching her to dive from the 10 metre platform. It's so exciting to watch her!

Different boards

There are two different kinds of diving boards — the springboard and the platform board. Springboards are set at either 1 m or 3 m above the water. They have more 'spring' than platform boards, allowing the diver to jump up into the air before coming back down towards the water. Platform boards are usually set at 5 m, 7.5 m and 10 m and are not so bouncy; divers already have enough height to perform acrobatic moves.

The starting position is one of the most important aspects of a good dive.

Tom Daley, Olympic bronze medallist at the 2012 Games, said of his training regime in that year: "I do ten sessions a week, five hours a day, and 60 per cent is spent doing weights, gymnastics and practising on a trampoline."

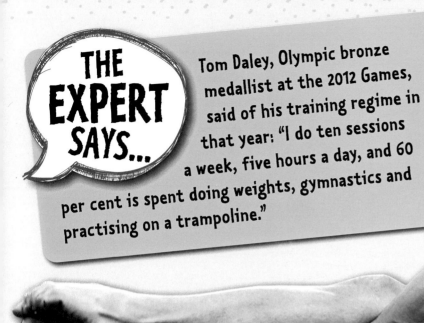

Tom Daly competing in China in 2014. Competitive diving is judged on technique in take-off, height, level of difficulty and the amount of splash on entry.

Basic positions

All dives consist of one or more of four basic positions: straight (body, arms and legs in a straight line), tuck (knees pulled up against the chest), pike (bent at hip but not at knees) and free (some kind of twist). The take-off may be backwards, or from a handstand position, head first or feet first. The flight part of the dive may involve a series of acrobatic manoeuvres, but the entry into the water must always be in a straight, vertical position.

top tip

Competitive divers put one hand over the other and flex their wrists just before entry so that they hit the water with the palm of one hand. This makes a 'hole' for the head and shoulders to follow and reduces the amount of splash, creating a 'rip' sound. That is why it is sometimes called a 'rip entry'.

Water polo

My friends and I play water polo whenever we can. Water polo is like handball, but in the water. You need two teams, each with six players plus a goalie who defends the team's goal net. The aim is to score as many goals as possible for your team. It helps if you're a strong swimmer and able to catch and throw a ball accurately with either hand. It's fast, energetic and great fun!

Players must practise throwing and catching the ball with either hand.

Swimming skills

Players other than the goalie are not allowed to touch the bottom of the pool during a game. They swim front crawl but keep their heads above water so that they can see what's going on, or swim backwards with their shoulders and head out of the water, or stay in one place by treading water. In a top-level match players may swim as much as three kilometres as well as holding and pushing each other to gain possession of the ball.

This goalkeeper stretches right out of the water to try to reach the ball.

No fouling!

The rules of water polo include the following:

- No touching the bottom of the pool (unless you are the goalie).

- The ball must be touched with one hand only (unless you are the goalie).

- No team can have possession of the ball for more than 30 seconds without shooting for the goal.

- Players can only push or hold another player if that player is in possession of the ball.

- Intentional splashing, blocking with two hands or holding back a player who does not have possession of the ball are all considered fouls.

CHECKLIST

What to wear?

☑ Players wear special caps that tie beneath the chin to protect the head and ears and to identify which team they are on – usually white or blue.

☑ Goalies wear red caps.

☑ Swimsuits or trunks are close fitting to make it harder for other players to grab hold of them.

☒ No goggles allowed!

Caps are essential for protection and for identifying members of your team!

top tip

The most efficient way to 'tread water' (in order to remain in one place) is to use the 'eggbeater' kick. Legs move in a circular motion, each leg alternating a sideways kick out from the knee. This gives stability when throwing the ball and strong swimmers can use it to force their bodies up out of the water for extra height.

Snorkelling and scuba

I tried snorkelling while I was on holiday by the sea last year. It's best when the water is clear, there are no waves and there's something interesting to look at, like fish or anemones. It took me a few minutes to get used to breathing through the snorkel, which is a tube that goes from your mouth up to the surface of the water. Once I got the hang of it, I loved exploring the shallows. I even saw a starfish!

A brightly coloured wetsuit or rash vest helps others to see you in the water. Flippers help you swim more efficiently.

Snorkelling

Snorkelling is a great sport if you like swimming in the sea. You can explore shallow water and spot underwater wildlife without the need for expensive equipment. Practise breathing with the snorkel in a swimming pool first and make sure you follow the same precautions for any open-water swimming. Follow safety advice, never snorkel alone and avoid areas where there are boats, windsurfers or jet skis.

Make sure you are comfortable with the snorkel and face mask before you swim in open water.

Scuba diving

Scuba diving is a highly skilled sport where the diver moves down below the surface of the water with the help of self-contained breathing apparatus. Beginner divers need lots of instruction before they can operate their equipment safely; usually this starts in a swimming pool. Children must be at least 10 years old before they can dive in open water and always need to be with a qualified adult. You should also be able to swim at least 200 metres and tread water for 10 minutes.

Scuba diving equipment looks heavy, but it is almost weightless underwater. In fact, divers often need to carry special weights to help them stay beneath the surface, because wet suits and diving cylinders give them extra buoyancy.

Scuba divers must always dive with a 'buddy'. They communicate with hand signals they've practised in advance.

top tip

There's so much to look at underwater! Just remember, underwater habitats such as coral reefs are incredibly fragile. They should never be touched or stepped on. Every diver must act responsibly to protect our amazing marine environment.

Swim for life

Swimming is the most amazing sport ever. It's great for building fitness and stamina. I love swimming competitively and relaxing at the pool with my friends. It's opened up new experiences like snorkelling and diving, and you can do it all year round. Best of all, it's great fun! I can't imagine a week without swimming!

Swimming makes you feel free!

THE EXPERT SAYS...

Prince William, patron of the English Schools Swimming Association and a keen water polo player, says: *"Swimming is unique. The ability to swim changes lives. It brings huge joy and it can keep us fit and healthy. But above all it can keep us safe."*

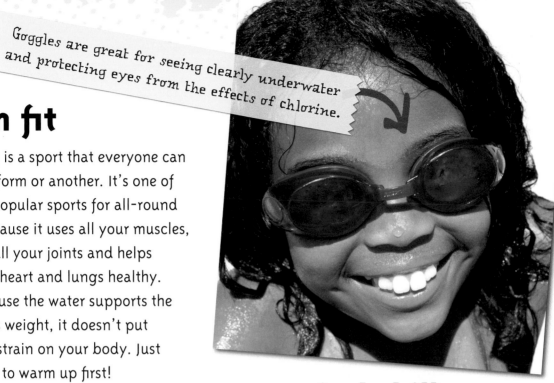

Goggles are great for seeing clearly underwater and protecting eyes from the effects of chlorine.

Swim fit

Swimming is a sport that everyone can do in one form or another. It's one of the most popular sports for all-round fitness because it uses all your muscles, exercises all your joints and helps keep your heart and lungs healthy. Also, because the water supports the swimmer's weight, it doesn't put too much strain on your body. Just remember to warm up first!

Before you can start to have windsurfing lessons, you need to be able to swim well.

Vital skills

Swimming is a great sport in itself, but becoming a confident swimmer is also a vital first step in many other sports such as water polo, sailing, windsurfing and kayaking. Swimming helps you and those around you stay safe around water. It is a skill that will last your whole life.

top ★ tip

There are so many ways to have fun and learn new skills in the water. Perhaps you'd like to try synchronised swimming, often known as synchro? Synchro is a rapidly developing sport that mixes swimming with gymnastics and dance in group formation in the water. See if there's a club near you!

Quiz

How mad about swimming are you? Try this quiz and find out!

1. How many swimming strokes are recognised in competitive swimming?

(a) 3;

(b) 4;

(c) 5?

2. Why is it best to keep splash to a minimum when doing the flutter kick?

(a) you'll soak the lifeguard;

(b) the kick has no power when your leg is out of the water;

(c) it doesn't look very elegant.

3. How far might a water polo player swim during the course of a match?

(a) 3 km;

(b) 5 km;

(c) 10 km.

4. What is a medley race?

(a) where the swimmer can choose which stroke they swim;

(b) a race in open water;

(c) where all four strokes are swum in turn.

5. How many kicks should you do in a single backstroke arm rotation?

(a) 5-7;

(b) 7-9;

(c) 3-5.

6. What kind of dive is a pike?

(a) where the diver is streamlined like a fish;

(b) where the diver is bent at the hips;

(c) where the diver begins with a handstand.

7. Which of the following kicks do you use to swim breaststroke?

(a) flutter kick;

(b) dolphin kick;

(c) frog kick.

8. Which of the following is the ONLY indication that it is safe to swim at the beach?

(a) clear sunny weather;

(b) information from the lifeguards;

(c) a calm sea.

Glossary

buoyancy Ability to float

chlorine A chemical that is added to the water in a swimming pool to kill germs.

coach A teacher who advises on training and fitness.

current The underwater pull of the sea or a river — often not visible on the surface.

dolphin kick The kick used in the butterfly stroke where both legs kick in a single movement.

drag Resistance in the water that slows a swimmer down.

eggbeater kick When legs kick with an alternating, circular movement to keep the swimmer afloat and in one place.

flutter kick A fast, loose kick with the legs extended — used for front crawl and backstroke.

freestyle A race where swimmers choose their stroke; usually, front crawl.

glide The movement of the body through water as the result of previous action such as a racing dive, a turn or a stroke.

lifeguard Someone trained in life-saving skills with expert knowledge of the swimming environment.

medley A race where all four strokes are swum in turn.

meet A swimming competition

pike Where the body is bent at the hips.

racing dive A fast, low, powerful dive into the water at the start of a race.

relay Where a team of swimmers take it in turns to finish the course.

rip entry A dive entry with minimal splash.

scuba Stands for Self-Contained Underwater Breathing Apparatus.

snorkelling Swimming underwater with a snorkel tube to allow flow of air from mouth to surface.

stamina The strength to keep swimming or exercising for long periods.

stroke A single rotation of the arm during swimming

synchro Synchronised swimming — a combination of gymnastics and swimming in the water, performed as a pair or a team.

tumble turn An underwater turn used during front crawl where the feet, not the hands, touch the wall.

Index